AGING ABUNDANTLY™

AGING ABUNDANTLY™

A Little Book of Hope

Dorothy Sander

Just when the caterpillar thought her world was over, she became a butterfly.

ISBN: 978-1-304-56398-9

Aging Abundantly Press, LLC
Durham, NC 27712

www.agingabundantly.com

Printed in the United States of America

CHANGE

We all know somewhere deep inside ourselves that we were put on this earth for a reason. We have a perpetual longing to know what that reason is and to find its meaning and purpose. We want to be assured that we have not lived in vain. But how do we discover this reason, this meaning, and this purpose when the ground keeps shifting beneath our feet?

Change is a natural part of life. In our youth we look upon change as exciting and energizing, as it is filled with new beginnings, opportunities and hope. Even if we are intimidated, we are able to struggle through with a deep sense of hope for new and better things to come.

The life changes that takes place between the ages of forty five and sixty five, are quite different. They are more about endings and loss, with a deep sense that there is much more loss in our future. It is no wonder we find ourselves in turmoil and out of sync with who and what we thought ourselves to be. We are in the process of going through a death and re-birth, a metamorphisis of a different kind than we've experienced before.

We are thrust into a period of life that is also rich with opportunity, it's just a different sort of opportunity, and one we are not used to looking for.

Midlife transitions, while difficult and often painful, provide us with the richly fertile ground required for a significant change in our perspective and modus operendi. The more difficult the transition, the more significant the change that can result.

As we let go of the drive, ambition, and expectations of our youth, we find we have a perfect opportunity to reach for deeper meaning, to ferret out our life's purpose, and to find a sense of direction that will carry us through our remaining years. We can then begin the writing of one of our final chapters.

As our focus shifts away from our children, our aging parents, and/or our careers, there is more space in our days and in our psyches to reflect on what has been and to examine our priorities. When I came face-to-face with myself at this time, I found I was no longer comfortable with the life I had chosen, and maybe more important, not chosen.

This was a painful and tumultuous period of time in my life, but I was strongly motivated by my discomfort to take a deeper look at what had led me to the place I found myself. It was time to evaluate again the ideas and concepts that I had perhaps inherited or borrowed and decide which of them I wanted to keep and which I would discard. It was now or never to live a life that was of my choosing. I was ready to look through the lens of my own camera, not one of another individual or culture.

I believed I had done all the rebelling I needed to do in my teens, twenties, thirties, and even forties. I had expected to coast as I aged. I realize now that forming a separate identity that allows us to soar with the angels (and butterflies) takes a lifetime. To fly higher, we must go deeper.

Finding our way through the maze of disintegration and reformation required for significant personal growth is an important task at midlife. Our transformation from a caterpillar to a butterfly is the task at hand. There is no point in burying our head in the sand or turning away from the transformation, for it will only reappear again later with ever-increasing urgency.

Struggling to break free from our chrysalis requires sustenance and support. I found just such help in the words and thoughts of great writers and thinkers both living and dead. These people understood bits and pieces of my struggles and shed light on areas needing attention. I felt less alone, strangely nudged forward and comforted at the same time.

I began to gather these quotes and share them with other midlife travelers on www.AgingAbundantly.com. I added, and continue to add, to my collection, as the same simple yet profound truths emerge over and over again. These quotes are a beacon in the night sky, and I want to share them with you.

I intentionally created a book that could be carried in your pocket or purse so that it might be a comforting companion in difficult times. I've included several blank pages at the end of the book where can add your own thoughts and/or more quotes. Your truth is the most important thing to carry with you.

My hope for you is that you will always find the courage to break free from your chyrsallis and dare to fly with the butterflies.

When your inner voice and vision is louder and more profound than the thoughts and opinions of those on the outside, you've begun to master life.
Unknown

If we go slowly and steadily, go where our hearts desire, find ways to get back to places we love, do the things we love to do—
slow and steadily, magic happens.
Martha Beck

A vision is not just a picture of what could be; it is an appeal to our better selves, a call to become something more.
Rosabeth Moss Kanter

I never panic when I get lost.
I just change where it is I want to go.
Rita Rudner

Clinging to the past is the problem.
Embracing change is the solution.
Gloria Steinem

Very often a change of self is needed more than a change of scene.
Arthur Christopher Benson

Look at everything as though you were seeing it either for the first or last time. Then your time on earth will be filled with glory.
Betty Smith

Truth is tough. It will not break,
like a bubble, at a touch, nay, you may kick
it all about all day like a football, and it will
be round and full at evening.
Oliver Wendell Holmes

All my life I used to wonder what
I would become when I grew up.
Then, about seven years ago, I realized that
I was never going to grow up—that growing
is an ever ongoing process.
M. Scott Peck

The process of metamorphosis is scary
and sometimes painful, but is also the way
to experience wonderful new adventures
we weren't even able to imagine
in our "caterpillar identities".
Accept the process: care for yourself,
dream big, work hard, and keep learning.
Then don't be surprised when one morning,
you wake up to find that you have wings.
Martha Beck

Things do not change; we change.
Henry David Thoreau

Just let go. Let go of how you thought
your life should be, and embrace the life
that is trying to work its way
into your consciousness.
Caroline Myss

BEAUTY

"What does it mean to be a woman when the beauty of my youth is fading?"

"How can I still consider myself feminine and attractive as a woman when my skin is sagging and wrinkles crease my eyes?"

"Does my life partner still find me desirable? How can I believe it? Do I still care?"

We struggle with what it means to be "beautiful" as we age.

As young women, our external beauty was everything to us. We believed it was essential for finding and securing a life partner. What now? Is it time to relinquish this enormous part of ourselves? Or is it time to look at our beauty in a different way?

Women seem to be genetically to desire to be beautiful. Like male birds, we strut our stuff to attract our mate, someone to father our children and protect us as we care for them. What now when beauty's purpose has faded?

Consider this:

Beauty

Kahlil Gibran

And a poet said, "Speak to us of Beauty."

Where shall you seek beauty, and how shall you find her unless she herself be your way and your guide?

And how shall you speak of her except she be the weaver of your speech?

The aggrieved and the injured say, "Beauty is kind and gentle.

Like a young mother half-shy of her own glory she walks among us."

And the passionate say, "Nay, beauty is a thing of might and dread.

Like the tempest she shakes the earth beneath us and the sky above us."

The tired and the weary say, "beauty is of soft whisperings. She speaks in our spirit.

Her voice yields to our silences like a faint light that quivers in fear of the shadow."

But the restless say, "We have heard her shouting among the mountains,

And with her cries came the sound of hoofs, and the beating of wings and the roaring of lions."

At night the watchmen of the city say, "Beauty shall rise with the dawn from the east."

And at noontide the toilers and the wayfarers say, "we have seen her leaning over the earth from the windows of the sunset."

In winter say the snow-bound, "She shall come with the spring leaping upon the hills."

And in the summer heat the reapers say, "We have seen her dancing with the autumn leaves, and we saw a drift of snow in her hair."

All these things have you said of beauty.

Yet in truth you spoke not of her but of needs unsatisfied,

And beauty is not a need but an ecstasy.

Beauty is not in the face;
beauty is a light in the heart.
Kahlil Gibran

Although beauty may be in the eye of the beholder, the feeling of being beautiful exists solely in the mind of the beheld.
Martha Beck

People don't remember the mistakes you have made or dark images you hold about yourself. They remember your beauty when you feel ugly; your wholeness when you are broken; your innocence when you feel guilty; and your purpose when you are confused.
African Saying

Let the beauty we love be what we do.
Rumi

A thing of beauty is a joy forever:
its loveliness increases;
it will never pass into nothingness.
John Keats

A woman whose smile is open and whose expression is glad has a kind of beauty no matter what she wears.
Annie Roiphe

Beauty is whatever gives joy.
Edna St. Vincent Millay

Flowers... are a proud assertion that a ray of beauty outvalues all the utilities of the world.
Ralph Waldo Emerson

People are like stained-glass windows.
They sparkle and shine when the sun is out,
but when the darkness sets in,
their true beauty is revealed only
if there is a light from within.
Elisabeth Kubler-Ross

Beauty is in the eye of the beholder
and it may be necessary from time to time
to give a stupid or misinformed
beholder a black eye.
Miss Piggy

_As we grow old…
the beauty steals inward.
Ralph Waldo Emerson

The more we learn to communicate with our bodies, the more we may feel as though we're aging backward, like Merlin the Magician, becoming healthier and more time.
Martha Beck

No matter how plan a woman may be,
if truth and honesty are written
across her face, she will be beautiful.
Eleanor Roosevelt

FEAR

Living in fear takes the joy from our days and the texture and richness from our lives. When we feel the nudge of fear, it's easy to succumb to the urge to huddle in a corner of our hearts and refuse to venture forth.

A day doesn't go by that we don't hear of, or live through, some natural or unnatural disaster. We are privy to unrelenting destruction at the hands of our fellow human beings. How do we feel secure? How do we keep finding the courage, day after day, to turn our faces to the sun?

The surest way to break through the barrier of fear is to acknowledge and accept that true courage can only come from within. As we learn, step by step, to turn to ourselves instead of the world for security and courage, we begin to see that something far greater than our fears exists, and that something is ready and waiting to carry us through.

Externals may physically defeat us, but our spirit can and will live on in spite of the disintegration of worldly things. Our bodies may fade, but all that is good lives on in all that is and was and will forever be.

Soak in the truth of the words spoken here and be fortified. You are stronger than you know. You have more courage than you ever believed possible.

Our deepest fear is not that we are inadequate. Our deepest fear is that we are powerful beyond measure. It is our light, not our darkness that most frightens us. We ask ourselves, Who am I to be brilliant, gorgeous, talented, fabulous? Actually, who are you not to be? You are a child of God. Your playing small does not serve the world. There is nothing enlightened about shrinking so that other people won't feel insecure around you. We are all meant to shine, as children do. We were born to make manifest the glory of God that is within us. It's not just in some of us; it's in everyone. And as we let our own light shine, we unconsciously give other people permission to do the same. As we are liberated from our own fear, our presence automatically liberates others."

Marianne Williamson

You gain strength, courage, and confidence by every experience in which you really stop to look fear in the face. You must do the thing which you think you cannot do.
Eleanor Roosevelt

No, I don't think that every fear is rational and all fears are good.
I feel fear is neutral—it's how we channel it that makes it good or bad.
Scott Young

Getting over your fear without doing anything scary is like learning to swim before you go near the water—it would be nice if such a thing were possible, but it ain't.
Martha Beck

We must build dikes of courage
to hold back the flood of fear.
Martin Luther King, Jr.

Put your desires above your fears. Stop running and face it, whatever it is.
Martha Beck

Most of us live two lives.
The life we live, and
the unlived life within us.
Between the two stands Resistance.
Steven Pressfield

Real life isn't always going to be perfect
or go our way, but the recurring
acknowledgement of what is working
in our lives can help us not only to survive
but surmount our difficulties.
Sarah Ban Breathnach

Remember that it's okay to ask for help
when you're stumped, because
sometimes you really can't be expected
to handle everything alone.
Martha Beck

There are some things one can only
achieve by a deliberate leap in the opposite
direction. One has to go abroad in order to
find the home one has lost.
Franz Kafka

Fears are educated into us, and can,
if we wish, be educated out.
Karl Augustus Menninger

The enemy is fear. We think it is hate;
but, it is fear.
Gandhi

When you say or do anything to please,
get, keep, influence, or control anyone or
anything, fear is the cause
and pain is the result.
Byron Katie

COURAGE

We can live our dreams. They are within our reach. No matter what our age or circumstance, we can find joy in our todays. We may have to give our dreams some breathing room or allow them to change shape a bit to fit our circumstances, but we do not have to abandon them or give up hope.

What we do have to do is give up fear and despair. There are always a hundred-and-one reasons why we really don't want to do the thing we think about doing. I'm the queen of negative thinking: ask my husband!

I always wanted to write, since the first time I held a pencil in my hand. I didn't begin to take that dream seriously until I was fifty. Since that time, my dream has shifted and changed with circumstances, but I am now doing what I love to do. It's not perfect. Nothing is, but the value of pursuing your dreams comes not from the dream itself, but from living from your heart, from the place where all dreams reside.

We all lack confidence to some degree or another. The bigger our hope, the harder it may be to risk. May of us experienced childhoods that weakened us rather than giving us the freedom to learn and expand. Our life experiences may have caused us to shrink even further.

We can choose courage. We can choose to walk away from despair, hopelessness, defeat. We can soldier on and reach way down deep inside and grab just the tinest corner of a dream that still remains beneath the wreckage. We can hold on for dear life until bit by bit the dream finds its way to the surface of our life.

We simply have to make the decision to try, to take the leap of faith. Just do it, one step at a time. There are no mistakes in life. There are only experiences from which we learn and move on, and every accomplishment begins with the decision to try.

Hold tight to your dreams. Let them be the beacon that guides you through the storm.

Life's up and downs provide windows of opportunity to determine your values and goals. Think of using all obstacles as stepping stones to build the life you want.
Marsha Sinetar

Let things come to you and be confident that everything will come when the time is right.
Byron Katie

Courage is like a muscle.
We strengthen it with use.
Ruth Gordon

Every passing minute is another chance to turn it all around.
from Vanilla Sky

Go confidently in the direction of your dreams. Live the life you've imagined.
Henry David Thoreau

There came a time when the risk to remain tight in the bud was more painful than the risk it took to blossom.
Anais Nin

If one advances confidently in the direction of one's dreams, and endeavors to live the life which one has imagined, one will meet with a success unexpected in common hours.
Henry David Thoreau

Life shrinks or expands in proportion to one's courage.
Anais Nin

Whoever is happy will make others happy too. He who has courage and faith willnever perish in misery.
Anne Frank

There has never been, and never will be, anyone who sees, thinks, or responds exactly the way you do. Whether you're revolutionizing physics or making a quilt, you must display your differences to make a difference.
Martha Beck

Courage is resistance to fear, mastery of fear, not absence of fear.
Mark Twain

Trusting in yourself, not what you accomplish is the key to success.
Deepak Chopra

I can be changed by what happens to me, but I refuse to be reduced by it.
Maya Angelou

Pursue your dreams not because you're immune to heartbreak, but because your real life, your whole life, is worth getting your heart broken a few thousand times.
Martha Beck

If you've lost focus, just sit down and be still. Take the idea and rock it to and fro. Keep some of it and throw some away and it will renew itself. You need do no more.

Clarissa Pinkola Estes

Courage is the most important of all virtues, because without courage you can't practice any other virtue consistently. You can practice any virtue erratically, but nothing consistently without courage.
Maya Angelou

Courage, it would seem, is nothing less than the power to overcome danger, misfortune, fear, injustice, while continuing to affirm inwardly that life with all its sorrows is good; that everything is meaningful even if in a sense beyond our understanding; and that there is always tomorrow."
Dorothy Thompson

Sometimes courage is the quiet voice
at the end of the day saying,
I will try again tomorrow.
Radmacher

Many of our fears are tissue paper thin,
and a single courageous step
would carry us clearn through them.
Brendan Frances Behan

TIME

Every day we have a choice to dwell in the past or focus on today. Ask yourself: what can I do today to bring me one step closer to my dream?

You do have today . . . this moment . . . now. You owe it to yourself to make the most of it.

Life goes by so quickly. I remember the moment I turned around and as if in a flash, my kids were grown. I am nearing sixty, and yet age is just a number to me.

I do not feel old. I don't feel sixty, but what does sixty feel like? Surely not this! My body shows the effects of time, but I often forget to notice.

Moving from fifty to sixty has been challenging, but mostly in my head. It is very unlike anything I had imagined. It has also been extraordinarily fulfilling.

Like most mothers, I cried when my kids left home, and like most daughters, I cried when my father died and then again when my mother died. I churned with regret. I felt as though I had wasted my youth, but then again, we all know "youth is wasted on the young."

I lived in fear of the future even longer, but through hard work and the invaluable support of friends and books, I ventured onto a path that feels like mine. It is not always obvious or blissful, but it *is* amazing, and many mornings it's quite definitely worth getting up for.

Life is richer now. My dreams are more meaningful and feel more attainable. We have today. I have today. *You* have today. Let's make the best of it and wake up tomorrow one step closer to the heart and soul that is us.

Whomever it is you were born to be,
whatever your soul was coded to
accomplish, whatever lessons you were
born to learn, now is the time
to get serious and get going.
Marianne Williamson

You must live in the present,
launch yourself on every wave,
find your eternity in each moment.
Henry David Thoreau

Empty time is a powerful medicine that
can make us more joyful and resilient,
but it's strangely hard to swallow.
Martha Beck

The great thing about getting olderis
that you don't lose
all the other ages you've been.
Madeleine L'Engle

If you start a day without a clear plan about
how you're going to spend your attention,
you'll end up wasting most of it.
Martha Beck

Time does not change us. It just unfolds us.
Max Frisch

While you might be feeling a bit depressed
that you are no longer young, you're
ecstatic that you're no longer clueless.
Marianne Williamson

Time is the coin of your life. It is the only coin you have, and only you can determine how it will be spent. Be careful lest you let other people spend it for you.
Carl Sandburg

If we take care of the moments,
the years will take care of themselves.
Maria Edgeworth

An unhurried sense of time is
in itself a form of wealth.
Bonnie Friedman

The secret of health for both mind and body is not to mourn the past, worry about the future, or anticipate troubles, but to live in the present moment wisely and earnestly.
Buddha

Both young children and old people have a lot of time on their hands. That's probably why they get along so well.
Jonathan Carroll

I must govern the clock,
not be governed by it.
Golda Meir

The future is something which everyone reaches at the rate of 60 minutes an hour, whatever he does, whoever he is.
C.S. Lewis

DECISION

Life demands much from each of us. It doesn't matter whether we are doing what we love to do or have found ourselves in circumstances we hate. We still must face each day, look fear and uncertainty in the eye, and move forward. If we refuse, we cannot claim to be truly alive.

Our path is seldom clear, even if we have an inkling of direction. The water is just murky enough to give us pause.

Whether we are someone who forges ahead with gusto or one who plods along, agonizing over each step, the course is the same. Choices must be made: simple, complex, insignificant, or monumental.

Each decision, one after another, chosen consciously or not, determines who we have been, who we are, and who we will be tomorrow. Our lives are the sum total of our choices, for better or worse.

Most of the time there are no clear, right-or-wrong decisions, just shades of gray that we squint with our mind's eye to discern. I wonder what would happen if instead of squinting, trying to "see the answer," we closed our eyes and listened instead. Might we hear the voice of our heart, where our true answers lie?

When our eyes are wide open, the noise of someone else's opinion or even an expert's advice may block out what is the answer for us.

Our direction can come only from the quiet voice that we too often bury in the noise of externals. Truth speaks more often in feelings and nuances than in bold statements. We must be utterly still to hear it.

Build your dreams upon the foundation of true desire, not on the subtle expectations of others that you have come to think of as your own.

It is in your moments of decision
that your destiny is shaped.
Anthony Robbins

Begin making choices based on
what makes you feel freer and happier,
rather than how you think an ideal life
should look. It's the process of feeling our
way toward happiness, not the realizing
of some Platonic ideal,
that creates our best lives.
Martha Beck

Perfectionism is a state of perpetual
victimization. Decision making is a state
of constant learning.
Thom Rutledge

When we let go of the constant attempts to
solve the content of our lives, and attend to
the important process of how we treat
ourselves and each other, we have a real
chance for peace of mind.
Thom Rutledge

Nothing ever goes away until it has taught
us what we need to know.
Pema Chodron

Those who desire to give up freedom in
order to gain security will not have, nor do
they deserve, either one.
Benjamin Franklin

The self is not something ready-made, but something in continuous formation through choice of action.
John Dewey

If you limit your choices only to what seems possible or reasonable, you disconnect yourself from what you truly want, and all that is left is a compromise.
Robert Fritz

The truth is that many people set rules to keep from making decisions.
Mike Krzyzewski

Life isn't about waiting for the storm to pass, it's about learning how to dance in the rain.
Unknown

Once you make a decision, the universe conspires to make it happen.
Ralph Waldo Emerson

The most difficult thing is the decision to act, the rest is merely tenacity. The fears are paper tigers. You can do anything you decide to do. You can act to change and control your life; and the procedure , the process is its own reward.
Amelia Earhart

SILENCE

Today is one of those wonderful rainy days that invite rest and reflection. Such a day is a rare occurrence for a cup-half-empty kind of person like me, and one to embrace.

On rare occasions, a rainy day and I co-exist happily together, feeding on our similar contemplative, brooding natures and snuggling under theocovers of introspection. A comfortable place I wish I could occupy more often.

It is a day that calls for a walk through puddles, or so my furry companion seems to be saying with his relentless prodding and pacing. He's a very determined creature, particularly when he has an agenda.

Not to be ignored, I sweatshirted, hooded, and leashed my furry companion, and together we ventured out into the pouring spring rain with eager determination. It was not long before I felt invigorated. The cool, moist air filled my lungs as my mind picked up pace to keep time with my footsteps. Uninhibited, all controls off, I could almost feel my thoughts involuntarily settle into a comfortable kind of sorting, like I do when I clear the clutter off the desktop of my computer. This goes here, that goes there, this can be discarded.

We came into rhythm, my brain and me, and it felt good! I don't give myself permission very often to take my hands and feet off the controls on my thoughts. Instead, I force myself to "focus" on one problem or another. Today, walking in the rain, letting my thoughts do what they needed to do felt good. Necessary. Liberating.

I often write about the benefits of a "quiet time." Today I learned the value of a different kind of quiet . . . one that consists of quieting my need to control my thoughts and disconnect from purposeful, guided brain activity, including a self-imposed quiet time. Sometimes the brain just needs to do some sorting!

I wonder how children who are subjected to mandated "quiet time" might react to the concept of "think time" instead. Would they be more cooperative and less resistant to stopping their activities if given something on which to focus their attention, even if it is their own thoughts? Wouldn't this be preferable to the arduous task of shutting down their eager little minds and bodies entirely, a task inordinately difficult for most?

Might teachers use this opportunity to instruct their students on how to tune in to their inner voice, the voice of their hearts, a beneficial life lesson? I can imagine children finding this an entertaining and amusing activity while achieving the same beneficial results as a quiet rest.

For weary adults, a long walk in the rain, without electronic attachments, is a perfect way to create an opportunity for "think time." We cannot always break away from the worry and planning and active thinking of our minds, but we can create space and time for the possibility that our thoughts might enjoy an opportunity to find their own path. What might we discover?

A DAILY DOSE OF PEACE

Begin

Begin today to connect to you and to the creative spirit that is your life force. Step by step, moment by moment, be still and rest in the beautiful creation that is you.

Quiet

Quiet is a soothing balm for some, while it can be a terrifying void for others. No matter where you are on the continuum, you are where you are supposed to be. Just begin.

Add a small dose of quiet to your day, *every*day that you can, whether it is simply a few minutes in the car after you've turned off the engine and before you enter the house or while sitting on your porch in the sun after dinner. Find a time and a place to just breathe.

Breathe in the stillness. Breathe in the clarity that quiet can provide. Connect with whatever it is that feels like the center of your being.

Build on this. Add five minutes, or ten, until you are comfortable and connected with a place you know is you . . . a place where you can hear the still, small voice of your heart.

Beauty

Take in the beauty around you. If there is none, create some by closing your eyes and imagining. Dwell on a beautiful flower, a masterful painting, a lyric in a poem, a melody that lifts your spirits. Absorb beauty in all its magnificence.

Replace the stress and the violence of the news with the lilt of Enya's* melodies. Assemble the most beautiful photos you can find and place them where you will see them often. Whenever possible, seek beauty first.

The beauty that touches you is within you. If you feel moved to create, create from the beauty that lives and breathes within you. The act of creation connects us to ourselves and is the very core of the dreams we've yet to uncover.

Rest

Rest deeply, fully, completely. Stop the forward motion of your mind and body. Put aside that one-more-thing that you think you *must* do . . . and rest. Sleep, if that is what comes. Sit. Read. Listen. Turn down the volume of your thoughts in any way you can. Busy your hands with needlework if you must, but make sure that what you do with your hands creates. If you can, go away from your day-to-day demands to a place that nurtures your soul—the beach, a mountainside cabin, a library or a bookstore. For an hour, a day, or a week, whatever is possible, whatever the deep fatigue and disconnect within you requires. You will know. Turn off the demands and rest.

SILENCE

The best way to break through any barrier
is to access a point of perfect stillness
at the center of your being, a self deeper
than your senses or your mind.
Martha Beck

Sitting quietly, doing nothing, spring comes
and the grass grows by itself.
Zen Proberb

Take as much stuff off your plate
as possible, so you can focus on doing
what's important, and doing it well.
Leo Babuta in Zen to Done

Attention is a powerful nutrient.
It amplifies and accelerates the situations
on which it is focused.
Martha Beck

The quieter you become,
the more you can hear.
Baba Ram Dass

There is a place in you
where there is perfect peace.
There is a place in you
where nothing is impossible.
There is a place in you
where the strength of God abides.
A Course In Miracles

If we have not quiet in our minds,
outward comfort will do no more for us
than a golden slipper on a gouty foot.
John Bunyan

When you rest in quietness and
your image of yourself fades,
and your image of the world fades,
and your ideas of others fade, what's left?
A brightness, a radiant emptiness
that is simply what you are.
Adyashanti

Just become quiet, still, and solitary, and
the world will offer itself to you
to be unmasked; it has no choice.
It will roll in ecstasy at your feet.
Dana Hawksister

Traditionally we are taught,
and instinctively we long, to give
where it is needed--and immediately.
Eternally; woman spills herself away
in driblets to the thirsty, seldom being
allowed the time, the quiet, the peace,
to let the pitcher fill up to the brim.
Anne Morrow Lindbergh

Quiet minds cannot be perplexed
or frightened, but go on in fortune or
misfortune at their own private pace,
like a clock during a thunderstorm
Robert Louis Stevenson

The question we need to ask ourselves
is whether there is any place we can stand
in ourselves where we can look at all
that's happening around us without
freaking out, where we can be quiet enough
to hear our predicament, and where we can
begin to find ways of acting that are at least
not contributing to further destabilization.
Ram Dass

True silence is the rest of the mind; it is to
the spirit what sleep is to the body,
nourishment and refreshment.
William Penn

We need quiet time to examine our lives
openly and honestly . . . spending quiet time
alone gives your mind an opportunity to
renew itself and create order.
Susan L. Taylor

Peace comes from within.
Do not seek it without.
Buddha

Silence is a doorway
into the heart of reality;
to cultivate a silent heart
is to discover your deepest truth.
Nan Merrill

FORGIVENESS

To forgive is to set a prisoner free and discover that the prisoner was you.
Lewis B. Smedes

If you let go of the past and move with your dreams, it will always be enough.
Mike Dooley

Forgiveness can be more than an act of the moment; it can be a way of life.
Whitley Strieber

Always forgive your enemies -- nothing annoys them so much.
Oscar Wilde

The heart of a mother is a deep abyss
at the bottom of which
you will always find forgiveness.
Honore de Balzac

Forgiveness does not change the past, but it does enlarge the future.
Paul Boese

He who cannot forgive breaks the bridge over which he himself must pass.
George Herbert

Life is an adventure in forgiveness.
Norman Cousins

Forgiving is love's toughest work,
and love's biggest risk. If you twist it into something it was never meant to be, it can make you a doormat or an insufferable manipulator. Forgiving seems almost unnatural. Our sense of fairness tells us people should pay for the wrong they do. But forgiving is love's power to break nature's rule.
Lewis B. Smedes

Forgiveness is the fragrance the violet sheds on the heel that has crushed it.
Mark Twain

Forgiveness is a virtue of the brave.
Indira Gandhi

Forgiveness is like faith.
You have to keep reviving it.
Mason Cooley

When you hold resentment toward another, you are bound to that person or condition by an emotional link that is stronger than steel. Forgiveness is the only way to dissolve that link and get free.
Catherine Ponder

Return to the centre of your heart;
not your past.
Unknown

HOPE

It's not always easy to figure out why people do what they do, especially when that person is us. Despite our best efforts, we often find that we are forever getting off what we think is the "right track." We take carefully calculated steps when what we may really need to do is to go with our gut, not our mind. However, we are afraid to trust the directives of our heart and soul.

A study was done that can give us a clue into one of the reasons we may not trust ourselves. In this study, a group of babies who could crawl but not yet walk were placed on a glass platform. Part of the platform was on top of solid ground and part was extended out over open space, so that as the babies crawled forward, they crossed onto a glass floor that was transparent. As you may know, we are born with a fear of falling, and this design was used to assess the children's response in a frightening situation.

Across the room, the mothers of the babies were divided into two groups. One group was told to smile encouragingly at her child when he reached the open space. The other group was asked to frown and look fearful. Neither group was to speak.

In all instances, the babies whose mothers looked at them with encouragement and smiles continued out onto the transparent glass flooring despite the normal fear of falling. The other babies who were looking at the faces of frightened, worried mothers did not venture forth.

How our parents responded to us, even as early as infancy, either reinforced our fears or set us free. If your mother was particularly fearful, like mine, you may have received a multitude of signals that have made it difficult for you to move into dangerous territory with ease and confidence. This, however, does not mean you cannot do so. It just means you'll have to work a little harder at it. Recognizing that what we feel when faced with a new challenge is simply fear of the unknown can help give us the reassurance that we did not receive as children.

Our fears may take a variety of forms. They may even give us false messages about what we really want to do. We may mistake these messages for our inner voice. They are very powerful.

One easy way to tell if what you are hearing is fear or your inner voice is to ask yourself this question when making a decision about a step to take: Does this step "say yes to life"? Fear closes doors; it does not open them. Fear keeps us stuck. Saying yes moves us forward. Even if we realize in time that the step was not the right one, we will have learned something about ourselves in the process and grown in confidence.

HOPE

I believe above the storm the smallest
prayer will still be heard.
And I believe that someone in the great
somewhere hears every word.
From the song "I Believe"

You gain strength, courage, and confidence by every experience in which you really stop to look fear in the face.
You must do the thing which
you think you cannot do.
Eleanor Roosevelt

Hope is both the earliest and the most indispensable virtue inherent in the state of being alive. If life is to be sustained hope must remain, even where confidence is wounded, trust impaired.
Erik H. Erikson

The simple act of hopeful thinking can get you out of your fear zone and into your appreciation zone ~ a habit that can replace anxiety with happy participation.
Martha Beck

Start by doing what is necessary,
then do what is possible, and suddenly
you are doing the impossible.
St. Francis of Assisi

Far away there in the sunshine
are my highest aspirations.
I may not reach them, but I can look up
and see their beauty, believe in them,
and try to follow where they lead.
Louisa May Alcott

Hope is the thing with feathers that perches in the soul – and sings the tunes without the words – and never stops at all.
Emily Dickinson

When one door closes another door opens; but we so often look so long and so regretfully upon the closed door, that we do not see the ones which open for us.
Alexander Graham Bell

The great challenge of adulthood
is holding on to your idealism
after you lose your innocence.
Bruce Springsteen

If you only walk on sunny days
you'll never reach your destination.
Paulo Coelho

Expect to have hope rekindled. Expect your prayers to be answered in wondrous ways. The dry seasons in life do not last. The spring rains will come again.
Sarah Ban Breathnach

The very least you can do in your life is to figure out what you hope for. And the most you can do is live inside that hope.
Barbara Kingsolver

If I keep a green bough in my heart, the singing bird will come.
Chinese Proverb

Everything that is done in the world is done by hope.
Martin Luther

Listen to the mustn'ts child. Listen to the don'ts. Listen to the shouldn'ts, the impossibles, the won'ts. Listen to the never haves, then listen close to me . . . Anything can happen, child. Anything can be.
Shel Silverstein

You may say I'm a dreamer, but I'm ot the only one. I hope someday you'll join us. And the world will live as one.
John Lennon

Hope Smiles from the threshold of the year to come, Whispering 'it will be happier'..."
Alfred Tennyson

Hope is sweet-minded and sweet-eyed. It draws pictures; it weaves fancies; it fills the future with delight.
Henry Ward Beecher

PURPOSE

Childhood is a magical time. In spite of the "slings and arrows of outrageous fortune," innocent beings see life differently. A child has an enormous curiosity, endless good will, hope that won't quit, and complete faith in life. The years may whittle away our innocence and undermine our confidence in life, but I have come to believe that the gifts we were given at birth remain with us far beyond childhood. They have simply gone underground for safekeeping until such time that we can once again appreciate them and put them to good use.

As a child, I lived in the magnificent state of Maine. It was pure heaven for a kid like me. Building snow forts and sucking on icicles were among my favorite pastimes in winter . . . catching polliwogs and climbing to the top of an enormous rock with my best friend or having a picnic in the woods were my summertime delights. I was too young to realize Maine was the freezing cold backwoods of hell for my mother. It was home to me, and I loved it.

I didn't brood on unpleasant things. What I faced as a child would seem monumental to me as an adult. Health issues, loneliness, the drudgery of day-to-day life in school, and how difficult it was to be painfully shy. I didn't lose myself to self-pity, or pay too much attention to the sadness I later recognized as my response to my position in my family of origin. Instead, I found my peace when I could in the woods and streams and by drawing enormous yellow suns on the whitest paper I could find. I created what warmth I could and allowed it to shine down on me from its thumbtacked place on the wall where it kept me warm despite the coldness in my days.

Children are amazingly resilient creatures. We can benefit from taking a moment to get reacquainted with the one that still lives inside of each of us. Perhaps if we take a few moments to look back on our younger years and roust that innocence from its long winter of hibernation, we might find the remnants of our authentic selves and the strength and wisdom that still reside within us. The hope and joy that comforted us then might just be what we need to face life's challenges today.

As a child, I knew the face of God, though He did not have a name. I trusted implicitly the outstretched arms of protection that held me securely when I rested in the hollow of an enormous tree. I soaked up the comforting aroma of peace from the woodsy smell of nature, and the force of hope inspired me as I watched day after day as an enormous icicle grew steadily on the corner of our little house until it reached the ground. I soaked up with amazement the charity and benevolence of nature, mesmerized by the continuous drip, drip, drip of maple syrup as it flowed from the little tube my Dad inserted into our maple tree. I rested in the unending peace that comforted me as I lay in my mother's lap on Sunday mornings, listening with my whole being to the echo of reverence as it seeped unannounced into my soul and the sweet scent of flickering candles lulled me to sleep. I knew God then. Only I have changed.

Find out who you are and do it on purpose.
Dolly Parton

Your purpose is that something
you express in everything you do.
It's your reason for existence.
Jonathan Mead

Dreams pass into the reality of action.
From the actions stems the dream again;
and this interdependence produces the
highest form of living.
Anais Nin

I have come to the conclusion that as much
as we may think we want life to be easy and
to be fed like babies - whether that's by food
companies or the entertainment industry -
we all have a desire for something more.
Natalie Holmes

How wonderful it is that nobody need wait
a single moment before starting
to improve the world.
Anne Frank

Too far, and too much", are excuses we
have all overcome when what we needed to
do mattered more than the excuse we held!
Dõv Baron

None of your pain has been pointless and
no part of your life has been wasted.
Martha Beck

It is good to have an end to journey
towards; but it is the journey that matters,
in the end.
Ursula K. Le Guin

The need to find meaning...is as real as
the need for trust and for love,
for relations with other human beings.
Margaret Mead

The world needs dreamers and the world
needs doers. But above all, the world needs
dreamers who do.
Sarah Ban Breathnach

Pursue some path, however narrow
and crooked, in which you can walk
with love and reverence.
Henry David Thoreau

If you believe you can, you probably can.
If you believe you won't, you most assuredly
won't. Belief is the ignition switch that gets
you off the launching pad.
Denis Waitley

People often say that motivation doesn't
last. Well neither does bathing - that's why
we recommend it daily.
Zig Ziglar

Our lives begin to end the day we become
silent about things that matter.
Martin Luther King, Jr

Life has no meaning in itself,
but only in the meaning we give it.
Like the clay in the artist's hands,
we may convert it into a divine form or
merely into a vessel of temporary utility.
Lama Anagarika Govinda

Passion is energy. Feel the power that
comes from focusing on what excites you.
Oprah Winfrey

Your beliefs become your thoughts.
Your thoughts become your words.
Your words become your actions.
Your actions become your habits.
Your habits become your values.
Your values become your destiny.
Mahatma Ghandhi

If your actions inspire others to dream more,
learn more, do more and become more,
you are a leader.
John Quincy Adams

"But try," you urge, "the trying shall suffice;
The aim, if reached or not, makes great
the life: Try to be Shakespeare,
leave the rest to fate!"
Robert Browning

If you don't know where you're going,
any road will get you there.
Lewis Carroll

CREATIVITY

Confusion is the welcome mat
at the door of creativity.
Michael J. Gelb

Thought is the sculptor who can create the
person you want to be.
Henry David Thoreau

People often say that this or that person
has not yet found himself.
But the self is not something one finds;
it is something one creates.
Thomas Szasz

There is within each of us the possibility
of magnificence. Every moment is
an opportunity to make it manifest.
Marianne Williamson

The very motion of our life
is towards happiness.
Dalai Lama

Happiness is not an ideal of reason,
but of imagination.
Immanuel Kant

Imagination is more important than
knowledge. Knowledge is limited.
Imagination encircles the world.
Albert Einstein

The power is in you. The answer is in you.
And you are the answer to all your
searches: you are the goal.
You are the answer. It's never outside.
Eckhart Tolle

Live out of your imagination, not your past.
Stephen Covey

Creativity comes from trust.
Trust your instincts.
Rita Mae Brown

Creativity is a shapechanger.
One moment it takes this form,
the next that. It is like a dazzling spirit
who appears to us all, yet is hard to
describe for no one agrees on what
they saw in that brilliant flash.
Clarissa Pinkola Estes

Within every woman there is a wild
and natural creature, a powerful force, filled
with good instincts, passionate creativity,
and ageless knowing.
Clarissa Pinkola Estes

Courage is the price that life exacts
for granting peace.
Amelia Earhart

Take time to listen to the music . . .
and ignite the melody of your soul.
D.J. Sander

And those who were seen dancing
were thought to be insane by those
who could not hear the music.
Frederich Nietzsche

Music is the language of the spirit.
It opens the secret of life
bringing peace, abolishing strife.
Kahlil Gibran

When we neglect the artist in ourselves,
there is a kind of mourning that goes on
under the surface of our busy lives.
Pat Schneider

Every artist dips his brush in his own soul,
and paints his own nature into his pictures.
Henry Ward Beecher

Art is a personal act of courage,
something one human does that creates
change in another.
Seth Godin

Anxiety is part of creativity,
the need to get something out,
the need to be rid of something or
to get in touch with something within.
David Duchovny

A hunch is
creativity trying to tell you something.
Frank Capra

ATTITUDE

When you judge another, you do not define them, you define yourself.
Dr. Wayne Dyer

A positive attitude may not solve all of your problems, but it will annoy enough people to make it worth the effort.
Herm Albright

The only disability in life is a bad attitude.
Scott Hamilton

If you have not slept, or if you have slept, or if you have headache, or sciatica, or leprosy, or thunder-stroke, I beseech you, by all angels, to hold your peace, and not pollute the morning.
Ralph Waldo Emerson

The secret of staying young is to live honestly, eat slowly, and lie about your age.
Lucille Ball

Think of yourself as a problem solver not a collection of problems.
Thom Rutledge

A single gentle rain makes the grass many shades greener. So our prospects brighten on the influx of better thoughts.
Henry David Thoreau

Being powerful is like being a lady. If you have to tell people you are, you aren't.
Margaret Thatcher

Whenever you become intensely focused on changing someone else's behavior, you might want to check what part of your own business you're avoiding.
Martha Beck

Angry people want you to see how powerful they are… loving people want you to see how powerful you are.
Chief Red Eagle

If you want to fly, you have to give up the things that weigh you down.
Unknown

Act as if what you do makes a difference. It does.
William James

When there is no enemy within, the enemies outside cannot hurt you.
African proverb

If you don't like something, change it. If you can't change it, change your attitude.
Maya Angelou

We cannot become what we want to be by remaining what we are.
Max DePree

SUCCESS

Getting what one wants in life seems not only possible, when we are young, but inevitable. In my youth, even in my darkest moments I believed with utter fervor and commitment that *if* I worked hard enough and *if* I did the right things, I would have a fulfilling and meaningful life. I knew it would not be perfect, but it would be good enough.

Little did I know that I would be trapped by a mindset, passed down from generation to generation, that would keep me bound and guided by forces I could not see. Driven by a combination of habit, ego, and an immature idea of love and caring, I plowed through the first half of my life as if my days on earth were endless. It is crystal-clear to me now, now that I have *really* "come of age", that life is not what it seems when we are young!

When I woke up from a life that now seems like a bad dream, I was nearly paralyzed by the awareness that, in spite of fifty years of effort and determination, I was no nearer my original destination than I had been thirty years earlier. I felt as though I had wasted my life and that I had given it all away, keeping very little for myself.

My immediate response was to announce to myself and to anyone who would listen, "I'm done doing for everyone else. I'm done living my life for my children, my parents, my husband, my friends, my animals, my job! It's time for me!" Those who bothered to listen undoubtedly heard the panic in my voice and heard what I was really saying: "I'm running out of time! I need to pick up the pace!"

It has been almost ten years since my "mid-life crisis." I still battle some of the same false beliefs that pre-programmed my life, but the battle is fought with a little more wisdom . . . *and* compassion. One of my most important lessons can be summed up in this quote by Lyanla Vanzant: "The only way to get what you really want is to let go of what you don't want." We cling tenaciously to so many things in life, many of which have no real meaning or purpose in the overall scheme of things. These "things" keep us trapped, bound, and unhappy, whether they are material possessions, jobs, ideas, or concepts.

The "letting go" is not always simple, or easy, and it isn't a "once and done" kind of thing. To find a life of joy and meaning, we must let go over and over again. It is the only way to keep moving forward toward the life we were meant to live. The minute we begin to cling to something that does not bring joy and meaning to our lives, we can be certain that we are going away from our true selves instead of toward them. What drives us then is not passion, but fear or insecurity.

When we cling tenaciously to what we are doing, we use up the emotional and practical space we need to keep available for something better. Sometimes we heap another layer on top, trying to kill the pain and discomfort of living our wrong choices, by dousing ourselves in alcohol, material things, vacations, a new romance, and a myriad of other escape tools. By filling our days with placebos, from the hedonistic to quasi-spiritual, we simply muffle our fears and accomplish only temporary escape from a life of true joy and inner peace.

Gradually, day by day, we can let go of those things that do not make us happy, and fill the space with something that does. When it is not readily apparent what will fill the empty space, then embrace the silence and the uncertainty. When we sit with the discomfort, we allow possibilities that exist just beyond our current awareness to make themselves known.

The only way to get what you really want is to let go of what you don't want.
Iyanla Vanzant

Success is not the key to happiness. Happiness is the key to success. If you love what you are doing, you will be successful.
Albert Schweitzer

Empty pockets never held anyone back.
Only empty heads and
empty hearts can do that.
Norman Vincent Peale

The first step toward achieving excellence is imperfection.
Martha Beck

I'd rather have roses on my table,
than diamonds on my neck.
Emma Goldman

Success is liking yourself, liking what you do and liking how you do it.
Maya Angelou

Obstacles are those frightful things you see when you take your eye off the target.
Henry Ford

The ladder of success is best climbed by stepping on the rungs of opportunity.
Ayn Rand

When you dance, your purpose is not to get to a certain place on the floor. It's to enjoy each step along the way.

Wayne Dyer

The difference between success and failure isn't the absence of fear but the determination to pursue your heart's desires no matter how scared you are.
Martha Beck

It doesn't matter how long we may have been stuck in a sense of our limitations. If we go into a darkened room and turn on the light, it doesn't matter if the room has been dark for a day, a week, or ten thousand years -- we turn on the light and it is illuminated.
Sharon Salzberg

Belief in oneself is one of the most important bricks in building any successful venture.
Lydia M. Child

It is hard to fail, but it is worse never to have tried to succeed.
Theodore Roosevelt

I don't know the key to success, but the key to failure is trying to please everybody.
Bill Cosby

AUTHENTICITY

Today it's time for authentic "truth or dare."
Dare yourself to believe in your creativity,
wherever it may lead you.
Trust that where it leads is exactly
where you're supposed to be.
Sarah Ban Breathnach

Boredom is the root of all evil –
the despairing refusal to be oneself.
Soren Kierkegaard

So often time it happens,
we all live our life in chains,
and we never even know we have the key.
The Eagles, Already Gone

Always be a first rate version of yourself,
instead of a second rate version
of somebody else.
Judy Garland

What is uttered from the heart alone,
will win the heart of others to your own.
Johann Wolfgang von Goethe

Be yourself. Everyone else is already taken.
Oscar Wilde

It took me a long time not to judge myself
through someone else's eyes.
Sally Field

Constantly measuring ourselves against others sours and shortens our lives, robbing us of the very things we think it will bring: prosperity, love, inner peace, the knowledge that we're good enough.
Martha Beck

Be who you are and say what you feel because those who mind don't matter and those who matter don't mind.
Dr. Seuss

Ask yourself right now,
What's my own nature if I have no outside forces telling me who or what I should be? Then work at living one day in complete harmony with your own nature, ignoring pressures to be otherwise.
Dr. Wayne Dyer

Once you become Real you can't become unreal again. It lasts for always.
Margery Williams

Before speaking, consult your inner-truth barometer, and resist the temptation to tell people only what they want to hear.
Dr. Wayne Dyer

The priviledge of a lifetime is being who you are.
Joseph Campbell

At fifty, the madwoman in the attic breaks loose, stomps down the stairs, and sets fire to the house. She won't be imprisoned anymore.
Erica Jong

Beneath, around, even within the cacophonous chaos of your life disintegrating, something infinitely powerful and surpassingly sweet is whispering to you.
Martha Beck

Transcending labels that you've placed on yourself or that others have placed upon you opens you up to the opportunity of soaring in the now in any way you desire.
Dr. Wayne Dyer

Say, do, and be what you would if no one else were looking. It will be scary at first, but if you persist, there will come that liberating moment when you'll feel yourself sailing straight through your life's most inhibiting barriers without even feeling a bump.
Martha Beck

That inner voice has both gentleness and clarity. So to get to authenticity, you really keep going down to the bone, to the honesty, and the inevitability of something.
Meredith Monk

FRIENDSHIP

God gave us our relatives;
thank God we can choose our friends.
Ethel Watts Mumford

Those who love you are not fooled by mistakes you have made or dark images you hold about yourself. They remember your beauty when you feel ugly; your wholeness when you are broken; your innocence when you feel guilty; and your purpose when you are confused.
African Saying

Surround yourself with high-energy people. Choose to be in close proximity to people who are empowering, who appeal to your sense of connection to intention, who see the greatness in you, who feel connected to God, and who live a life that gives evidence that Spirit has found celebration through them.
Dr. Wayne Dyer

Honest disagreement is often a good sign of progress.
Mohandas K. Gandhi

A little Consideration, a little Thought for Others, makes all the difference.
Winnie the Pooh

When we are dreaming alone it is only a dream. When we are dreaming with others, it is the beginning of reality.
Dom Helder Camara

People come into your life for a reason, a season or a lifetime. When you figure out which it is, you will know exactly what to do.
Chris Moon-Willems

Remember, we all stumble, every one of us. That's why it's a comfort to go hand in hand.
Emily Kimbrough

No one can develop freely in this world and find a full life without feeling understood by at least one person.
Paul Tournier

Nobody needs a smile more than the one that cannot smile to others.
Dalai Lama

You cannot truly listen to anyone and do anything else at the same time.
M. Scott Peck

If you don't risk anything,
you risk even more.
Erica Jong

Conflict cannot survive without your participation.
Wayne Dyer

Good relationships are built on understanding, acceptance, and forgiveness ~ of ourselves and the one we love.
Dorothy Sander

The best method to break out of solitary confinement is to seek to understand others, and help them understand you.
Martha Beck

One of the oldest human needs is having someone to wonder where you are when you don't come home at night.
Margaret Mead

A single rose can be my garden…a single friend, my world.
Leo Buscaglia

Don't walk in front of me; I may not follow. Don't walk behind me; I may not lead. Just walk beside me and be my friend.
Albert Camus

A friend is a loved one who awakens
your life in order to free
the wild possibities within you.
John O'Donohue

A real friend is one who walks in when the rest of the world walks out.
Walter Winchell

JOY

Life itself is the proper binge.
Julia Childs

Work is not always required...there is such a thing as sacred idleness, the cultivation of which is now fearfully neglected.
George MacDonald

Life may not be the party we hoped for, but while we're here we should dance.
Author Unknown

There are exactly as many special occasions in life as we choose to celebrate.
Robert Brault

Joyfulness keeps the heart and face young. A good laugh makes us better friends with ourselves and everyone around us.
Orison Swett Marden

When we create harmony in our minds and hearts, we will find it in our lives. The inner creates the outer. Always.
Louise L. Hay

Don't postpone joy until you have learned all of your lessons. Joy is your lesson.
Alan Cohen

LOVE

The first duty of love is to listen
Paul Tillich

There are two ways of spreading light...to be the candle, or the mirror that reflects it.
Edith Wharton

To the world you might be one person, but to one person you might be the world.
Author Unknown

Wake at dawn with a winged heart and give thanks for another day of loving.
Kahlil Gibran

A hug is like a boomerang – you get it back right away.
Bil Keane

You never lose by loving. You always lose by holding back.
Barbara De Angelis

If you love somebody, let them go, for if they return, they were always yours. And if they don't they never were.
Kahil Gibran

No one can give you anything--love, shame, self-esteem--until y ou give it to yourself. Today, give yourself good things.
Martha Beck

Let there be spaces in your togetherness
and let the winds of heavens dance
between you. Love another but make not a
bond of love. Let it rather be a moving sea
between the shores of your souls.
Kahlil Gibran

Love is what we were born with.
Fear is what we learned here.
Marianne Williamson

My life is an indivisible whole,
and all my attitudes run into one another;
and they all have their rise in my insatiable
love for mankind.
Mohandas K. Gandhi

Being heard is so close to being loved
that for the average person
they are almost indistinguishable.
David Augsburger

Love sometimes wants to do us a great
favor: hold us upside down and
shake all the nonsense out.
Hafiz of Persia

Let us love, since our heart is made
for nothing else.
St. Therese

HAPPINESS

The path to enlightenment is not a path at all, it's actually a metaphor for the time it takes for you to allow yourself to be happy with who you already are, where you're already at, and what you already have – no matter what.
Mike Dooley

My life has no purpose, no direction, no aim, no meaning, and yet I'm happy. I can't figure it out. What am I doing right?
Charles Schultz

Happiness is something you decide on ahead of time.
Unknown

Happiness is when what you think, what you say and what you do are in harmony.
Mohandas Gandhi

Don't go through life, grow through life.
Eric Butterworth

Your life follows your attention. Wherever you look, you end up going.
Martha Beck

If you smile when no one else is around, you really mean it.
Andy Rooney

The Art of Happiness

There was never a time when so much official effort was being expended to produce happiness and probably never a time when so little attention was paid by the individual to creating the personal qualities that make for it. What one misses most today is the evidence of widespread personal determination to develop a character that will, in itself, given any reasonable odds, make for happiness. Our whole emphasis is on the reform of living conditions, of increased wages, of controls on the economic structure—the government approach—and so little on man improving himself. The ingredients of happiness are so simple that they can be counted on one hand. Happiness comes from within, and rests most securely on simple goodness and clear conscience. Religion may not be essential to it, but no one is known to have gained it without a philosophy resting on ethical principles. Selfishness is its enemy; to make another happy is to be happy one's self. It is quiet, seldom found for long in crowds, most easily won in moments of solitude and reflection. It cannot be bought; indeed, money has very little to do with it. No one is happy unless he is reasonably well satisfied with himself, so that the quest for tranquility must of necessity begin with self-examination. We shall not often be content with what we discover in this scrutiny. There is much to do, and so little done. Upon this searching self-analysis, however, depends the discovery of those qualities that make each man unique, and whose development alone can bring satisfaction. Of all those who have tried, down the ages, to outline a program for happiness, few have succeeded so well as William Henry Channing, chaplain of the House of Representatives in the middle of the last century: "To live content with small means; so seek elegance rather than luxury, and refinement rather than fashion; to be worthy . . . to study hard, think quietly, talk gently, act frankly; to listen to the stars and birds, to babes and sages, with open heart; to bear all cheerfully, do all bravely, await occasions, hurry never; in a word to let the spiritual, unbidden and unconscious, grow up through the common." It will be noted that no government can do this for you; you must do it for yourself.

William S. Ogdon

New York Times, Editorial Page, Dec. 30, 1945

GRATITUDE

Gratitude I had no shoes and complained, until I met a man who had no feet.
Indian Proverb

One can be thankful no matter how little they think they have, and with that gratitude comes personal power, responsibility, and the quiet confidence that what you have is all you need.
Sue Ann Crockett

Gratitude makes sense of our past,
brings peace for today,
and creates a vision for tomorrow.
Melody Beattie

Wake at dawn with a winged heart and give thanks for another day of loving.
Kahlil Gibran

As you breathe in cherish yourself. As you breathe out cherish all beings.
Dalai Lama

I am thankful for laughter, except when milk comes out of my nose.
Woody Allen

Gratitude changes the pangs of memory into a tranquil joy.
Dietrich Bonhoeffer

Gratitude unlocks the fullness of life. It turns what we have into enough, and more. It turns denial into acceptance, chaos to order, confusion to clarity. It can turn a meal into a feast, a house into a home, a stranger into a friend. Gratitude makes sense of our past, brings peace for today and creates a vision for tomorrow.
Melody Beattie

One looks back with appreciation to the brilliant teachers, but with gratitude to those who touched our human feelings. The curriculum is so much necessary raw material, but warmth is the vital element for the growing plant and for the soul of the child.
Carl Jung

In ordinary life we hardly realize that we receive a great deal more than we give, and that it is only with gratitude that life becomes rich.
Dietrich Bonhoeffer

Connection with gardens, even small ones, even potted plants, can become windows to the inner life. The simple act of stopping and looking at the beauty around us can be prayer.
Patricia R. Barret

WISDOM

Find your truth and live it in love and your legacy will unfold bit by bit to find its place in the tapestry of eternity.
D. J. Sander

Keep me away from the wisdom which does not cry, the philosophy which does not laugh and the greatness which does not bow before children.
Kahil Gibran

Wisdom comes with the ability to be still. Just look and just listen. No more is needed. Being still, looking and listening activate the non-conceptual intelligence within you. Let stillness direct your words and actions.
Eckhart Tolle

Always choose the irrational wisdom of the heart over the cold analysis of the mind.
Deepak Chopra

Wisdom enables us to see beyond ego and to gain clarity where there might otherwise be confusion.
Allan Lokos

Your vision will become clear only when you can look into your own heart. Who looks outside, dreams; who looks inside awakes.
Carl Jung

Honesty is the first chapter
in the book of wisdom.
Thomas Jefferson

Even if you are a minority of one,
the truth is the truth.
Ghandi

Old age is not a disease--it is strength
and survivorship, triumph over all kinds of
vicissitudes and disappointments,
trials and illnesses.
Maggie Kuhn

Those who dream by day are cognizant of
many things which escape those who
dream only by night.
Edgar Allan Poe

Ours is not the task of fixing the entire world
at once, but of stretching out to mend the
part of the world that is within our reach.
Clarissa Pinkola Estes

The best mind-altering drug is truth.
Lily Tomlin

The sould always knows what to do to heal
itself. The challenge is to silence the mind.
Caroline Myss

Wisdom grows in quiet places.
Austin O'Malley

ABUNDANCE

Give from your abundance and your well will never run dry.
D.J. Sander

The hope for abundance can sometimes make people put up with all kinds of stuff that hurts their spirit. Self love, trust, courage and the willingness to shake life up is sometimes needed in order to make and carry out whole being healthy choices.
Sylvia Brallier

Doing what you love is the cornerstone of having abundance in your life.
Wayne Dyer

Once you deliberately focus on abundance, you'll be overwhelmed by all the good things that show up like manna in the desert, without much effort on your part.
Martha Beck

The test of our progress is not whether we add more to the abundance of those who have much it is whether we provide enough for those who have little.
Franklin D. Roosevelt

Not what we have but what we enjoy, constitutes our abundance.
Epicurus

Abundance is not something we acquire. It is something we tune into.
Wayne Dyer

The world breaks everyone, and afterward, some are strong at the broken places.
Ernest Hemingway

The greatest good you can do for another is not just to share your riches but to reveal to him his own.
Benjamin Disraeli

If you want to live peacefully, joyfully and abundantly in the years to come, you must walk your talk.
Martha Beck

The butterfly counts not months but moments, and has time enough.
Rabindranath Tagore

Whatever we are waiting for - peace of mind, contentment, grace, the inner awareness of simple abundance - it will surely come to us, but only when we are ready to receive it with an open and grateful heart.
Sarah Ban Brathnach

MY FAVORITE QUOTES

I hope you will go out and let stories happen to you, and that you will work them, water them with your blood and tears and your laughter till they bloom, till you yourself burst into bloom.

Clarissa Pinkola Estes

If you enjoyed this book be sure to connect with Dorothy online.

www.AgingAbundantly.com
www.AgingAbundantly.wordpress.com
www.DorothySander.com

On Facebook:
ww.Facebook.com/AgingAbundantly

On Twiter: @AgingAbundantly

www.ingramcontent.com/pod-product-compliance
Ingram Content Group UK Ltd.
Pitfield, Milton Keynes, MK11 3LW, UK
UKHW020219250726
13967UKWH00001B/88

9 781304 563989